Little Miss Muffet counts to TEN

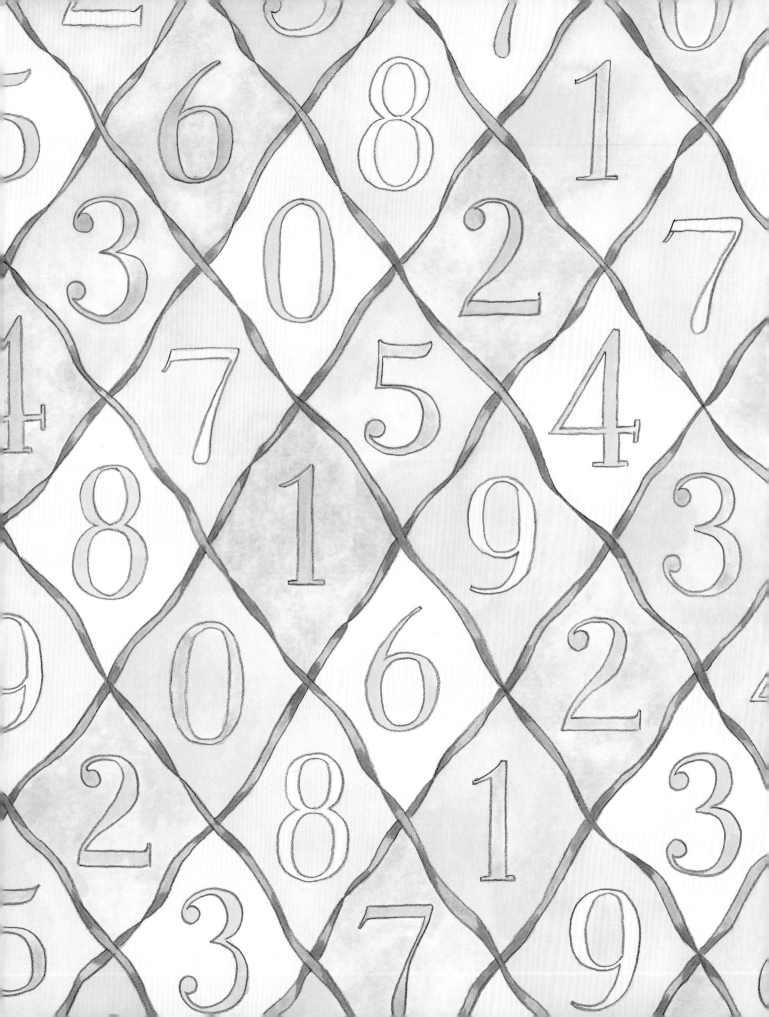

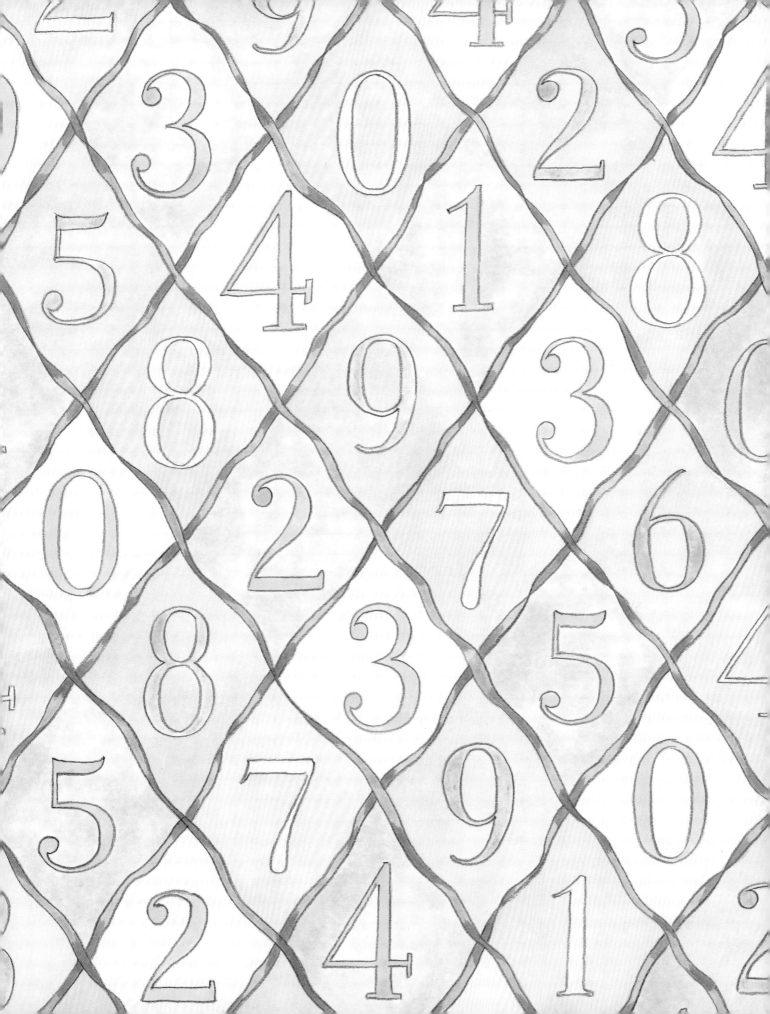

For Ottoline

A Red Fox Book

Published by Random House Children's Books
20 Vauxhall Bridge Road, London SW1V 2SA
A division of Random House UK Ltd
London Melbourne Sydney Auckland
Johannesburg and agencies throughout the world

1 3 5 7 9 10 8 6 4 2

First published in Great Britain by Andersen Press Ltd 1997

Red Fox edition 1999

Printed in Hong Kong

RANDOM HOUSE UK Limited Reg. No. 954009

ISBN 0 09 925609 6

Little Miss Muffet counts to TEN

Emma Chichester Clark

RED FOX

Little Miss Muffet
Sat on a tuffet,
Eating her curds and whey;
There came a big spider,
Who sat down beside her
And frightened Miss Muffet away.

Traditional nursery rhyme

1

Little Miss Muffet
Sat on a tuffet,
Eating her curds and whey,
When along came one spider
Who sat down beside her,
And said to Miss Muffet,
"Please stay!"

Little Miss Muffet
Sat on the tuffet,
Eating her curds and whey,
When along came two lemurs
With trumpets and streamers,
And bunting to make a display.

Little Miss Muffet
Sat on the tuffet,
Eating her curds and whey,
When along came three magpies
With taffeta bow-ties,
And waistcoats of very pale grey.

Little Miss Muffet
Sat on the tuffet,
Eating her curds and whey,
When along came four foxes
With neatly wrapped boxes,
And jellies lined up on a sleigh.

Little Miss Muffet
Sat on the tuffet,
Eating her curds and whey,
When along came five pussycats
With milkshake and party hats,
And small pots of chocolate soufflé.

Little Miss Muffet
Sat on the tuffet,
Eating her curds and whey,
When along came six poodles
With oodles of noodles,
And flutes which they started to play.

Little Miss Muffet
Sat on the tuffet,
Eating her curds and whey,
When along came seven bears
With a table and chairs.
They said, "We'll sit here, if we may."

Little Miss Muffet
Sat on the tuffet,
Eating her curds and whey,
When along came eight puffins
With blueberry muffins,
And each clutched a tiny bouquet.

Little Miss Muffet
Sat on the tuffet,
Eating her curds and whey,
When along came nine gibbons
With balloons tied with ribbons,
And bananas arranged on a tray.

Little Miss Muffet
Sat on the tuffet,
Eating her curds and whey,
When along came ten crocodiles
With a box and ten greedy smiles.
They saw her and shouted, "HOORAY!"

Little Miss Muffet
Jumped up from her tuffet;
She looked at the box in dismay.
Were they taking her back
In a box as a snack?
But she waited to hear what they'd say.

AND...

There was cheering and prancing,
And whooping and dancing -
And what did the crocodiles say?
"You have made a mistake;
We have brought you a cake!
Don't you know? It's your birthday today!"

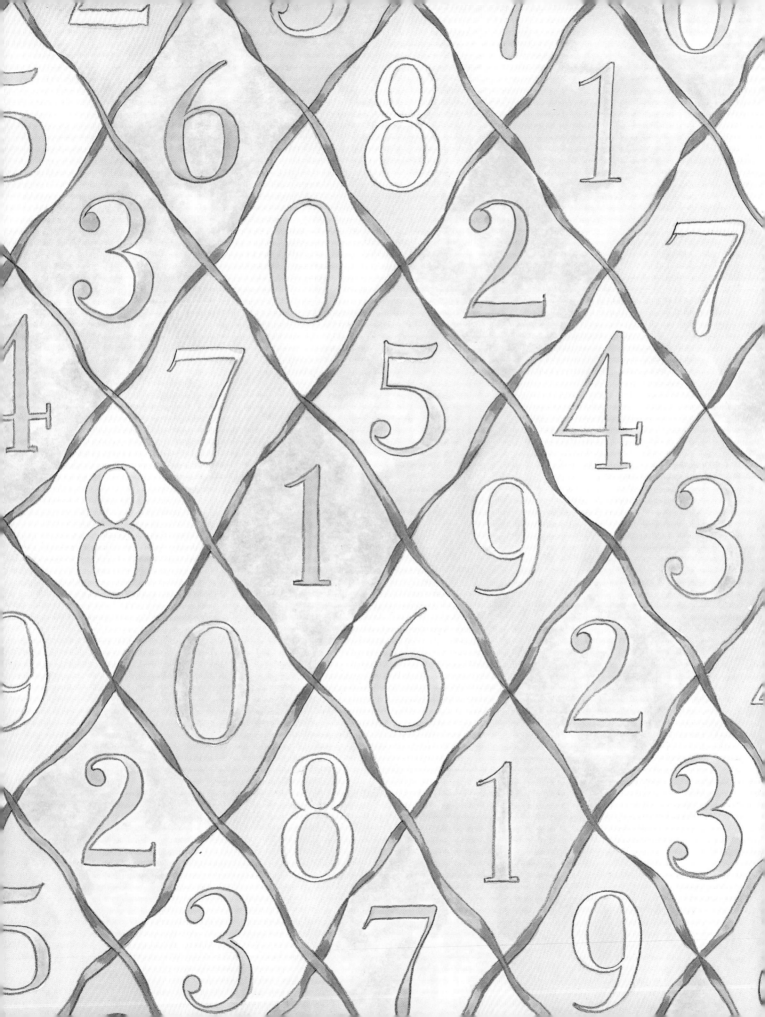

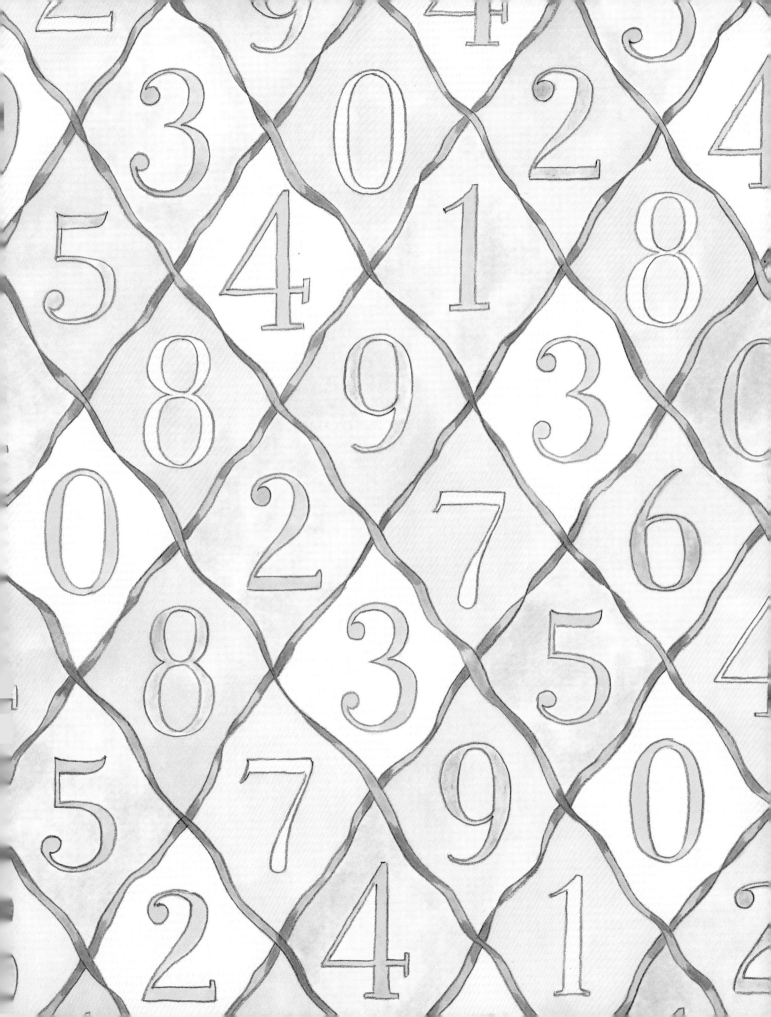

Some bestselling Red Fox picture books

THE BIG ALFIE AND ANNIE ROSE STORYBOOK
by Shirley Hughes
OLD BEAR
by Jane Hissey
OI! GET OFF OUR TRAIN
by John Burningham
DON'T DO THAT!
by Tony Ross
NOT NOW, BERNARD
by David McKee
ALL JOIN IN
by Quentin Blake
THE WHALES' SONG
by Gary Blythe and Dyan Sheldon
JESUS' CHRISTMAS PARTY
by Nicholas Allan
THE PATCHWORK CAT
by Nicola Bayley and William Mayne
WILLY AND HUGH
by Anthony Browne
THE WINTER HEDGEHOG
by Ann and Reg Cartwright
A DARK, DARK TALE
by Ruth Brown
HARRY, THE DIRTY DOG
by Gene Zion and Margaret Bloy Graham
DR XARGLE'S BOOK OF EARTHLETS
by Jeanne Willis and Tony Ross
WHERE'S THE BABY?
by Pat Hutchins